SCIENCE FUN WITH TOY BOATS AND PLANES

Rose Wyler
Pictures by Pat Stewart

JULIAN MESSNER • New York

Text copyright © 1986 by Rose Wyler
Illustrations copyright © 1986 by Pat Stewart

Published by Julian Messner, A Division of Simon & Schuster, Inc.
Simon & Schuster Building
Rockefeller Center
1230 Avenue of the Americas
New York, New York 10020

Lib. ed. 10 9 8 7 6 5 4 3 2 1

Pbk. ed. 10 9 8 7 6 5 4 3 2 1

JULIAN MESSNER and colophon are trademarks of Simon & Schuster, Inc.
Manufactured in the United States of America

Design by Lisa Hollander

Library of Congress Cataloguing in Publication Data
Wyler, Rose. Science fun with toy boats and planes. Includes index.
Summary: Easy experiments to do at home or school with home equipment, showing basic principles of how boats
float and move and how planes fly.   1. Science — Experiments — Juvenile literature.   2. Scientific recreations — Juvenile
literature.   3. Boats and boating — Juvenile literature.   4. Airplanes — Juvenile literature.
(1. Science — Experiments.   2. Experiments.   3. Boats and boating.   4. Airplanes)
Q164.W85 1985   629.04'6   85-8842
ISBN 0-671-55573-1   Lib. ed.
ISBN 0-671-62453-9   Pbk. ed.

ACKNOWLEDGMENTS

The author and publisher wish to thank the people who read the manuscript of this book and made suggestions: Lewis Love, Great Neck, New York, Public Schools; Dr. Richard Leigh, Brookhaven National Institute; Dr. Howard Wolko, National Air and Space Museum; Herman Schneider, Elementary Science Specialist; and the many young "helpers" who tried the experiments.

Other Books by Rose Wyler

The Giant Golden Book of Astronomy
Prove it!
Secrets in Stones [all written with Gerald Ames]
Real Science Riddles
Science Fun with Peanuts and Popcorn

FOREWORD

Science is a way of looking at the world around you and trying to understand how things work. Did you ever ask "Why is the sky blue?" or "Why does a seed begin to grow?" or "What is a cloud?" Nearly everyone asks such questions, but you can do more than that. You can do real science experiments to help you find the answers.

This book will show you how to do experiments that explain how boats and planes work. The experiments are easy to set up at home or at school and they are fun to do. As you do these experiments you will begin to think and work the way a scientist does.

Lewis Love
Great Neck Public Schools
Long Island, New York

CONTENTS

Hi, Captain!

What boat will you sail today? A sailboat? A paddle boat? Take the one you like. Sail it wherever you like—in a pond, in a pool, or in a tub.

Or do you want to fly a plane? What kind? A glider? A helicopter? A jet?

You can make all these boats and planes from things you find around the house. They are toys, of course. But they all work the way real boats and planes do. And you can use them in real science experiments.

This book tells you how.

Boats Afloat

It's easy to make a toy boat. Just take an empty milk carton and cut it in half. Use the half closed at both ends for the main part of your boat. That part is called the hull.

A piece of colored paper makes a nice sail. Punch three holes in it with a pencil.

Then run a soda straw through the paper. That makes the mast that holds up the sail. Stand the straw in the hull. Hold it in place with a dab of clay, or with tape that will stick when wet.

Any size milk carton can be used for a boat, but all the models shown are made from two-quart cartons.

Ask a grown-up to cut them for you.

Now set your boat afloat. Blow on it. Or fan it with a newspaper. How does it sail, Captain?

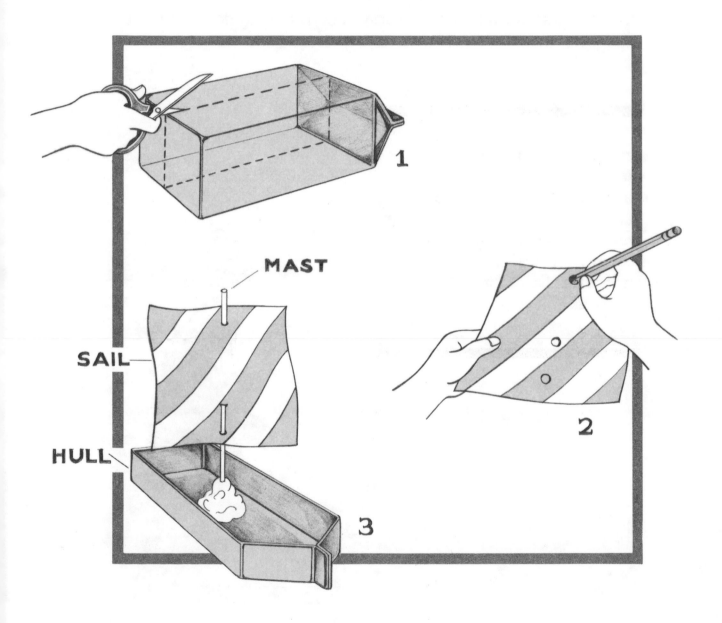

MAST

SAIL

HULL

1

2

3

See how high your boat floats. Why does it ride so high?

Water keeps pushing up against the hull. You can feel this push. Press down on the hull with both hands and you feel the upward push working against you. Stop pressing down and the hull bobs up.

Try this. Take an empty can and punch a hole in the bottom. Then lower the can into a tub of water. Water pushes up through the hole, making a fountain. Let go of the can and the water rises in it, until the can sinks.

Your boat would sink, too, if it leaked.

What Makes a Boat Sink?

Your boat is light, yet it has some weight. Because of its weight, it pushes down on the water. If the boat is loaded, it pushes down harder. If it pushes down harder than the water pushes up, the boat will sink.

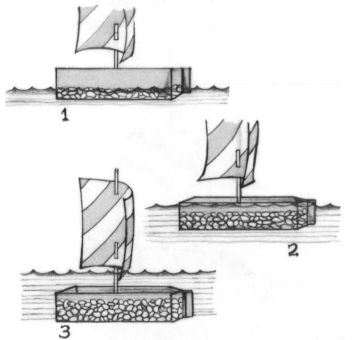

You can see how this happens. Load the boat with stones, adding one at a time. Watch the hull go farther and farther into the water. As the load gets heavier, the downward push gets stronger. Suddenly it is stronger than the water's upward push. Then down goes the boat.

S.O.S! S.O.S! That's the call for help at sea. It means SAVE OUR SHIP. Don't worry about the boat. Pull it up and let it dry. Soon it will be ready to sail again.

Balloon Rig

If you want your boat to carry a very heavy load, rig it with a balloon. Blow up the balloon and stick it on the hull with waterproof tape when the boat is dry. Now, how many stones can it carry? See how many more stones your boat can carry when you rig it with two balloons. Next try three balloons.

What do the balloons do? Rigged with balloons, the boat takes up more space. The boat displaces—that is, moves aside—more water. Then more water is pushing up against it, and the boat can carry a heavier load. The more water the boat displaces, the heavier the load it can carry.

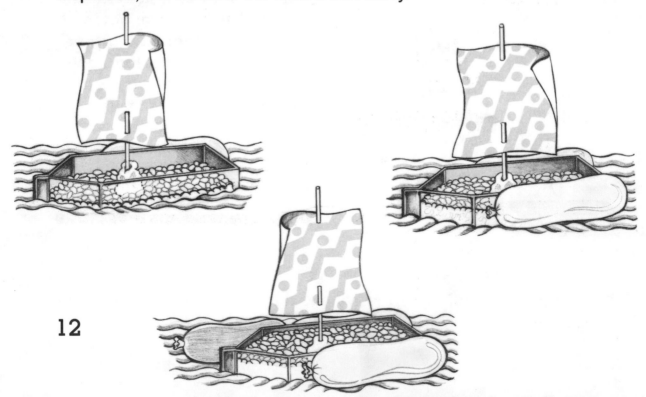

Perhaps you wonder why the boat's weight pushes down. Weight is due to gravity and gravity pulls everything downward, toward the earth. It pulls on water, too. Yet water pushes up on the boat. Water can do this because it flows. It is a liquid and can be displaced.

Weight and Floating

Like most people, you probably are too heavy to float. You start to sink when you lie on the water and stretch out your arms and legs. But if you take a deep breath, your chest swells. You displace more water—maybe another quart. Well, a quart of water weighs four pounds. Now the amount you displace weighs as much as you do. The water pushes up on you as hard as you push down on it—and you float.

The same rule holds for a boat, or anything else. It floats when its weight equals or is less than the weight of the water it displaces. If anything weighs more than that, it sinks.

From Ship to Shore

Will you sail your boat outdoors? Then you will need some way to keep it from drifting when it's not in use. If you can't tie it to a dock, you can drop an anchor.

For an anchor, use a metal nut. Tie it to three feet of string. Then stick the string on the front of the boat with waterproof tape. Keep the anchor in the hull until you are ready to drop it to the bottom of the pond.

Where will you go with your boat? Why not take a trip to Make-Believe Island? Load you boat with stones and pretend they are things for a picnic.

To go from ship to shore your sailboat needs a little boat. You can make one from aluminum foil and use a paper clip to hold it in place. Make some figures from modeling clay for passengers.

When the passengers get into the small boat, will you let them stand, Captain? Well—see what happens. Stand a clay figure in the small boat. When you set it afloat, it is top-heavy. The boat overturns. Quick to the rescue!

Steady and Ready

Set the boat afloat again. But this time make the "passengers" sit down. Now the boat is steady. Why is that?

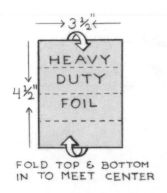

FOLD TOP & BOTTOM
IN TO MEET CENTER

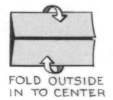

FOLD OUTSIDE
IN TO CENTER

CUT ON DOTTED LINES

FOLD ON DOTTED LINES

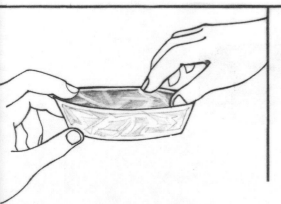

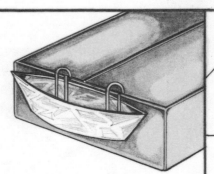

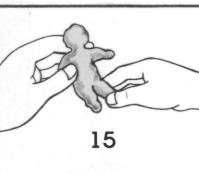

15

The weight of a boat, or anything else, seems to be centered at one point. This point is called the center of gravity. A boat is top-heavy and unsteady if its center of gravity is high above the bottom of the boat. The boat rocks, then settles with the center of gravity as far down as it can go. And that might mean the boat overturns.

When the figure stands in your small boat, the center of gravity is too high. That's why the boat goes down.

A tall, empty milk carton acts the same way when you stand it in a tub of water. The carton is top-heavy with a high center of gravity. The carton won't stay upright. Down it comes, bringing down the center of gravity.

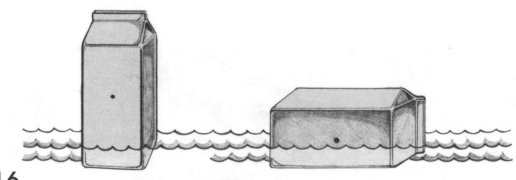

Watch the Waves

Your sailboat, with its flat bottom, has a low center of gravity. It doesn't rock much, not even when there are waves.

Waves are made by the wind or something that stirs the water. The water on top bounces up and down. This starts a ripple that starts another ripple that starts another ripple and so on. But the water itself doesn't move forward. If a boat is on a wave, it bobs up and down and rocks from side to side while staying in one place. If it moves forward, it is because of the wind.

See for yourself and make some waves in the bathtub, or in a pond. Stir the water with your hand and watch the boat ride the waves.

17

Sailing a Catamaran

If you like a fast boat, pick one with a V-shaped hull. The hull is streamlined, like a fish. Its shape cuts down friction —that is, the drag of the water against the boat. The only trouble is, a V-shaped hull is unsteady. But the unsteadiness can be overcome if two V-shaped hulls are used and tied together. This kind of boat is called a catamaran.

To make a catamaran, get a two-quart milk carton and ask a grown-up to help you cut it. First cut the carton diagonally across the top. Then cut it down the long edge to the bottom. From there cut diagonally across the outer edge.

Open the carton and fix the pointed ends so there are no loose flaps. Then use tape or staples to hold the ends in place. Add a sail and the boat is ready to go to sea.

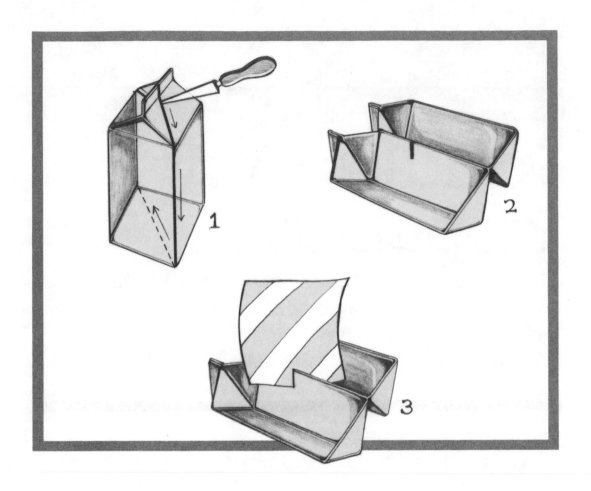

Make waves in the water and watch your catamaran ride them. How does it sail, Captain?

If you make another catamaran and cut it in half, you can see how the single V-shaped hull behaves. Put the hull in water and it rolls over to one side. Its center of gravity is too high. But you know how to change that—just put some weight in the bottom. All boats with one V-shaped hull are weighted down below.

Paddles and Propellers

Row, row, row your boat—and as you row, the oars push back water. That push makes the boat go forward. Power boats work in the same way. A paddle wheel or a propeller pushes back water, making the boat move the opposite way.

Paddle Power

You can see how a power boat works with a paddle wheeler that's made from a milk carton. Do you have another two-quart carton handy?

Ask a grown-up to cut the carton straight down the middle. Use one half for the hull. Cut a strip from the other half for the paddle. Then make a support for the strip with two pencils. Punch two holes into the rear of the hull and push the pencils in them so that their ends stick out about two inches. Slip a rubber band over the ends of the pencils and put the paddle in the loop. Now the boat is ready to be launched.

Twist the rubber band by twirling the paddle wheel *toward* you. Twist it around and around. As you set the boat afloat, let go of the paddle wheel. Splash. Dash. Off goes the boat. Watch the paddle wheel. It keeps turning *away* from you. Each time it hits the water, it pushes back water and that makes the boat move forward.

Now can you make the boat go backward?

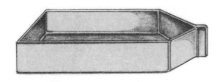

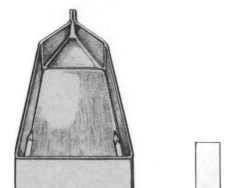

Action and Reaction. Why must water be pushed back to make a boat go forward? A push is a force—an action. Push against anything and it kicks back. It reacts. When a paddle pushes against water, the water kicks back against the paddle, driving the boat forward.

The first power boats had paddle wheels, driven by steam engines. Robert Fulton, who invented this kind of boat, got the idea when he was a boy. He and a friend often went fishing in a rowboat that they rigged with a pair of paddle wheels. The boys put one on each side of the boat and connected them with a rod. When they turned the rod the paddle wheels turned, and the boat moved along while the boys looked for fish.

You can put two paddle wheels on a boat, too—not on a big boat, but on a little one. Rig up another milk carton with two pencils and a rubber band. To fit the paddle wheels on it, make each one as shown in the picture:

Cut a square from a milk carton that is about 1-1/2 inches on each side. Next cut the square in half. Make a slit in each half in the middle of the long edge. Fit the slits into each other and you have a double paddle wheel. Now make another one like it.

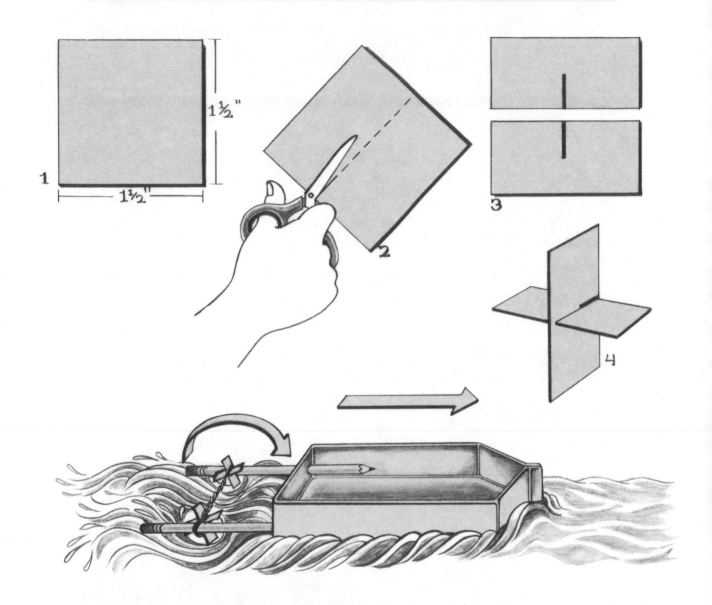

Slip both wheels in the rubber band loop of your boat. Twist the rubber band by turning a paddle. Let go of it as you float the boat. The water swirls and the boat speeds away. How fast it goes!

Is this boat faster than you other paddle wheeler? Have a race between them, and see which one wins.

23

Only a few old boats have paddle wheels now. Propellers that turn very fast drive the power boats in use today.

How a Propeller Works

A boat propeller is really a screw—one that works in water. Look at the thread on a wood screw. The thread goes round and round so that one edge after another can catch and push against the wood. On a propeller, the blades work like the thread of a screw. They are set at a slant so that first one, then another, will strike the water.

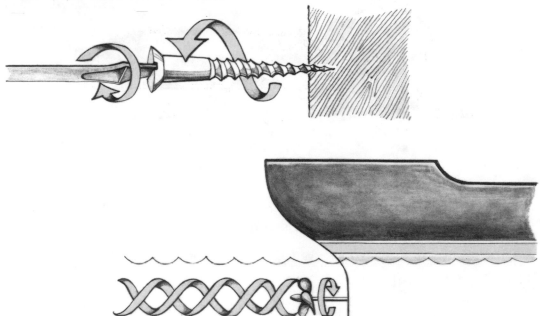

When a propeller turns, each blade pushes back some water. The water reacts by pushing the opposite way. That makes the boat go forward.

Do you have a toy boat with a propeller? Then try this experiment.

Start up the propeller and put the boat in a tub of water. Let a few drops of food coloring fall behind the propeller. Watch the colored water swirl. As the propeller pushes it back, the boat moves forward.

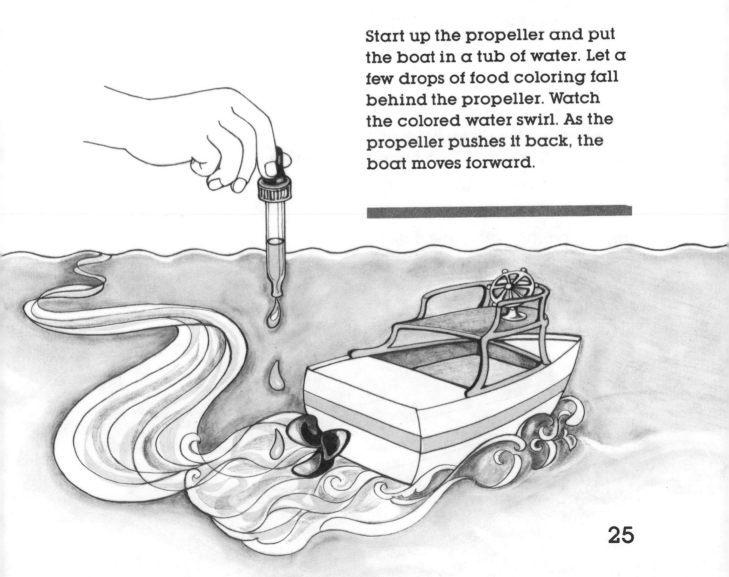

A Boat that Sails out of Water

There really is a boat that sails above the water. It's called the Hovercraft. It's a new invention, so perhaps you haven't seen one yet.

The Hovercraft moves over water on a cushion of air inside a rubber skirt. Pumps force air down into the cushion. The skirt swells until it looks like a huge tire. Then an airplane propeller on the deck starts to swirl, driving the craft forward on the air cushion. The air causes less friction than water. It cuts down drag, and the craft moves fast.

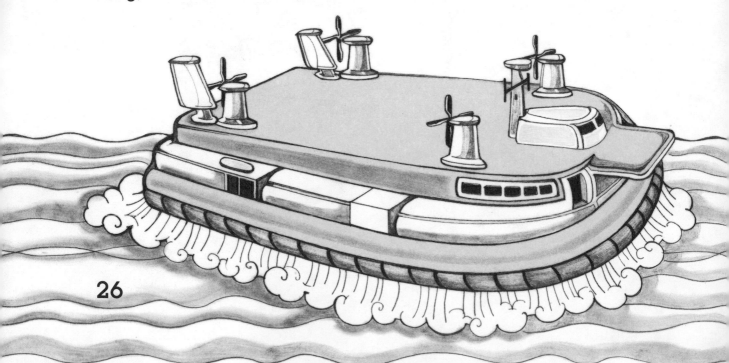

Here's a toy Hovercraft that you can make. It rides on air from a blown-up balloon, but it shows how the Hovercraft works.

You will need a plastic lid from a coffee can, a spool, a balloon that can be fitted over the spool, tape, and a tub of water. You will need a helper, too.

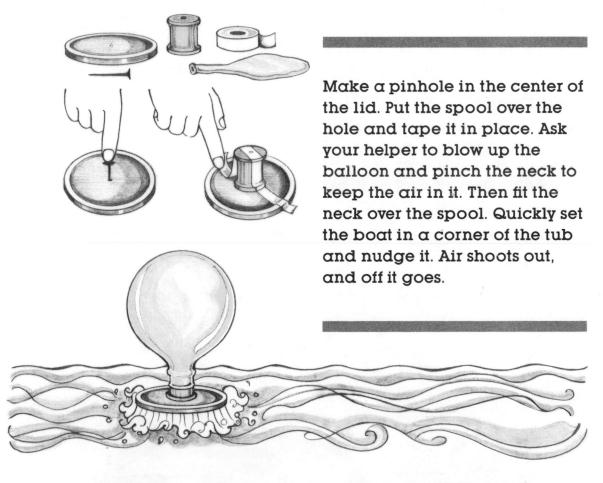

Make a pinhole in the center of the lid. Put the spool over the hole and tape it in place. Ask your helper to blow up the balloon and pinch the neck to keep the air in it. Then fit the neck over the spool. Quickly set the boat in a corner of the tub and nudge it. Air shoots out, and off it goes.

Will your toy Hovercraft also work on land? Try it on something smooth like glass. If it doesn't work, wipe salad oil around the rim, and try it again.

Floating without Water

It's possible to float across the United States—not in a boat, of course, but in a balloon. Floating in air is like floating in water. If a balloon, or anything else, weighs no more than the air it displaces, it stays up. This means it must be filled with a gas like helium, which is lighter than air.

At first hot air was used to fill big round balloons. Inventors hoped the balloons would be used for transportation, but people didn't think they were safe. Only those who were daring flew in them.

Later, propellers were put on huge, long balloons. Although a few of these giants flew across the Atlantic Ocean with passengers, airplanes soon proved to be faster and safer. Today balloons are used mainly for sport and to lift weather instruments.

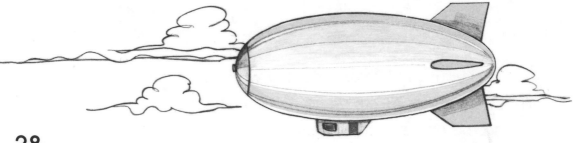

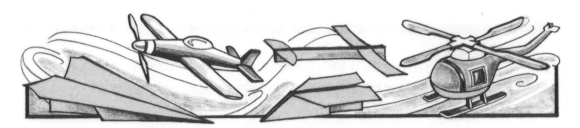

Up, Up into the Air

An airplane is much too heavy to float. It stays up only when the air moves swiftly over and under its wings. But people didn't know this when they first tried to fly. Some inventors built planes with wings that flapped like birds' wings. Others built huge kites and tried to fly in them. All crashed in a few seconds.

Still people kept trying to fly. Scientists began to experiment with air streams and test small plane models in wind tunnels. Then scientists built big gliders that stayed up, and they flew in them.

The next step was flying under power. The first ones to do this were the Wright brothers. They put a motor and a propeller on a glider they had built and in 1903, they flew in it. The plane stayed up less than a minute, but that minute marked the beginning of the Air Age.

The Wright brothers became interested in flying when they were boys. Their father had given them a little helicopter invented by a French scientist. The toy actually flew. As the boys played with it, they wondered if a plane with fixed wings would fly, too. But how would it stay up?

Years later, the Wrights learned the answer when they found out how air streams work. You can find out, too.

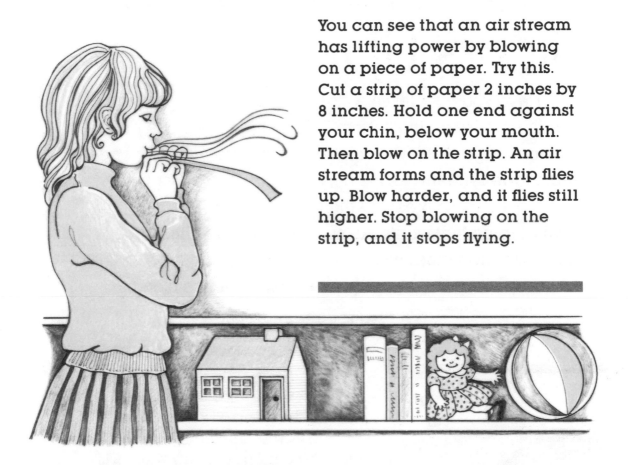

You can see that an air stream has lifting power by blowing on a piece of paper. Try this. Cut a strip of paper 2 inches by 8 inches. Hold one end against your chin, below your mouth. Then blow on the strip. An air stream forms and the strip flies up. Blow harder, and it flies still higher. Stop blowing on the strip, and it stops flying.

As air moves in a stream, it loses pressure. Pressure above the strip gets weaker than pressure below. This makes the strip fly up. The faster the air moves, the more pressure it loses. So the harder you blow on the strip, the higher it flies.

How an Airplane Stays Up

Have you ever taken a close look at an airplane wing? The top is curved; the bottom is flat. When the plane moves, the front edge of the wing divides the air into an upper stream and a lower stream. As the upper stream flows over the curved top, it loses more pressure than the lower stream. A strong upward force that works like suction develops. This force is called lift—and that's what it does. It lifts the big heavy plane and keeps it up in the air while the plane speeds along.

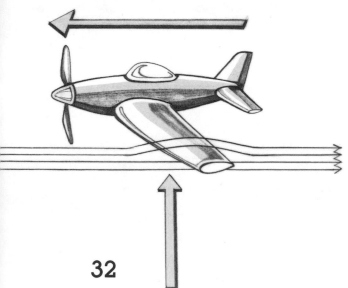

To see how a curved top helps lift a wing, try this. Take another strip of paper, 2 inches by 8 inches. Bring the ends together and hold them against your chin. Blow down on the paper and watch it rise. Does it come up higher than the flat strip?

Propellers that Work in Air

An airplane needs wings to fly, but the wings do not make it go. In a plane with a propeller, the propeller does this job.

An airplane propeller works like a screw. It also works like another wing—a wing with a twist. The front of the propeller is curved like the top of a wing. As air passes over the propeller, suction on the front of the propeller helps pull the plane through the air.

Look at the propeller of a model plane that flies, and you will see that the blades are curved. Spin the propeller, holding your hand in front of it. Then hold your hand in back of it. Which way does it throw the air? Backward?

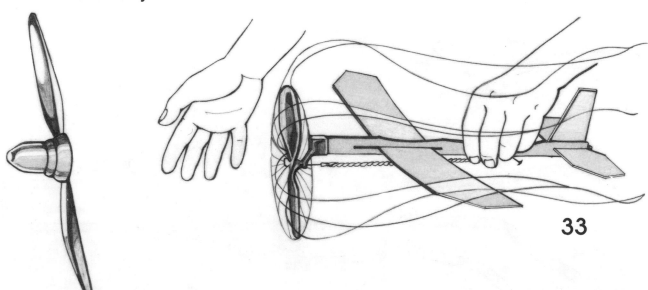

How Jets Drive a Plane

All the early planes had propellers, but now most planes are driven by jet engines. These engines suck in air, mix it with gasoline, then burn the mixture. Very hot gases form and push out through the tail pipe. The plane reacts, pushing forward.

A balloon reacts like a jet engine if you blow it up, and then let it go. As air rushes out of the neck, the balloon moves in the opposite direction.

All the while a plane is flying, it rubs against air. This friction causes drag and slows up the plane, just as friction from water slows up a boat. The more drag there is, the harder the engine must work to drive the plane forward.

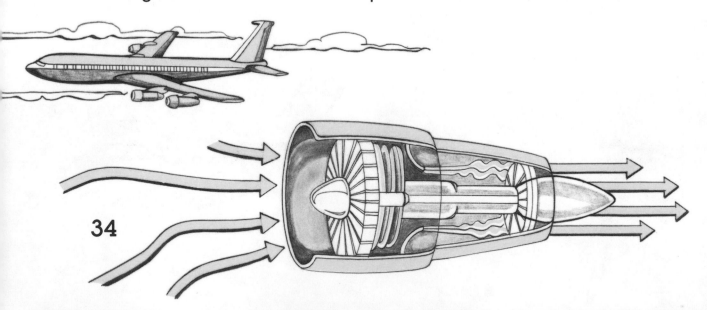

Streamlining

Planes, like boats, are streamlined to cut down drag. The nose is pointed or rounded so when it moves, it rubs against less air than a broad, flat nose. The body and wings of a plane also have shapes that cut down friction.

To see how different shapes move through the air, take two sheets of paper, the same size. Make a small ball of one; spread out the other so it's flat. Drop them both from the same height at the same time. The ball lands first, doesn't it?

More air touches the flat paper than the ball. So there's more friction against it as it falls. There's also a stronger upward push on it. As the paper pushes down on the air, the air reacts. It pushes up on the paper, slowing its fall.

A glider is a light plane that flies without an engine. You can test a glider, too. Here's one that's easy to make.

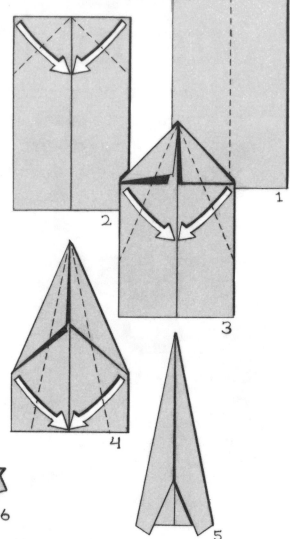

1. Take a piece of paper, 3 inches by 5 inches.
2. Fold it in half lengthwise.
3. Fold back the corners at one end and bring them to the center.
4. Fold back the same ends again and bring them to the center.
5. Fold back the ends once more, then bring them to the center.
6. Lift up the sides and there's your glider.

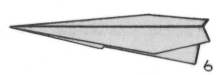

Now try this drop test.

In one hand, hold the glider with its nose pointing down. In the other hand, hold a flat piece of 3-by-5 inch paper. Stand on a chair and drop them both at the same time. Which lands first? The glider?

Models that Fly

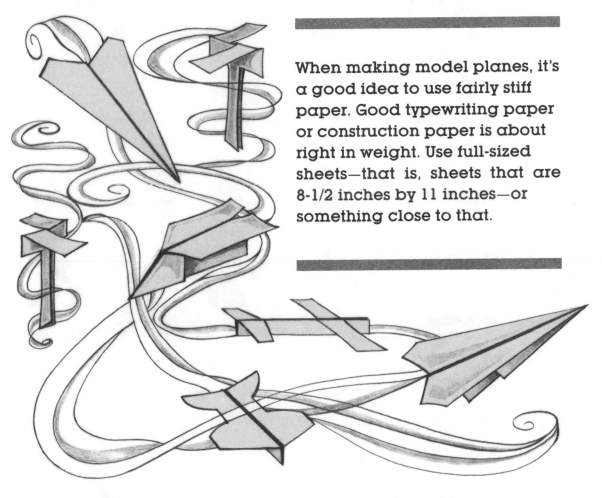

When making model planes, it's a good idea to use fairly stiff paper. Good typewriting paper or construction paper is about right in weight. Use full-sized sheets—that is, sheets that are 8-1/2 inches by 11 inches—or something close to that.

To start with, make a big glider from a sheet of typing paper. Shape it like the little test model. You will find that it goes quite far.

37

Flying a Glider

If you fly your glider outdoors and there is a breeze, face directly toward it. Hold the glider at eye level. Point the nose down slightly and push the glider forward to start it off. This push does the work of the engine.

How does the glider fly? If it comes down steeply, you may not be pushing hard enough to start it at the right speed. Speed is needed to make the air stream over and under the wings, and lift the glider.

GREENVILLE ANNUAL
PAPER PLANE CONTEST

Does the glider circle or nose dive? If it does either, it is not balanced well. Balancing a glider—or airplane—is like balancing a boat.

The glider has a center of gravity, and if the weight on each side is the same, the glider balances and stays level.

Test the glider with a paper clip near the tail, then with the clip in the middle, and then with the clip near the nose. Where must the clip be to make the glider balance? Or does the glider fly better without the clip?

Suzy's Special

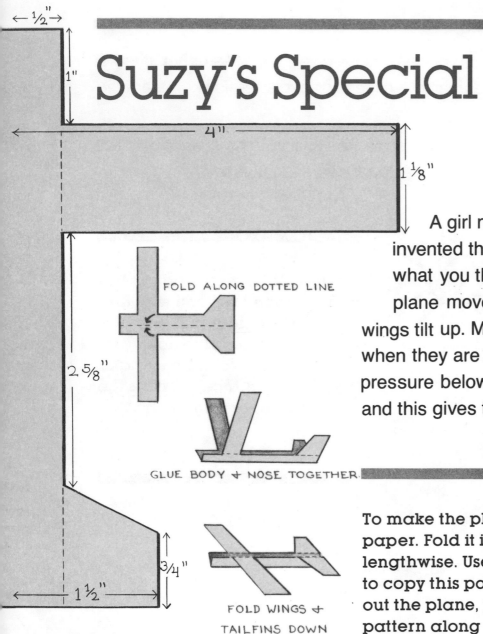

← ½" →

1"

4"

1 ⅛"

FOLD ALONG DOTTED LINE

2 ⅝"

GLUE BODY & NOSE TOGETHER

3/4"

← 1½" →

FOLD WINGS &
TAILFINS DOWN

A girl named Suzy invented this plane. See what you think of it. As the plane moves forward, the wings tilt up. More air hits them when they are level. Air pressure below the wing rises, and this gives the plane lift.

To make the plane, use stiff paper. Fold it in two lengthwise. Use tracing paper to copy this pattern. Then cut out the plane, putting the pattern along the folded side of the paper.

Glue the body and nose together. Spread the wings and tail fins and your plane is ready for a test flight.

Hold the body near the middle, pointing the nose upward a little. To drive the plane, give it a gentle thrust.

Does the nose go up? If it does, the plane needs more weight in front. Dab some modeling clay on the nose tip and test it again. Add or take away clay until the plane flies steadily. How far does it go?

41

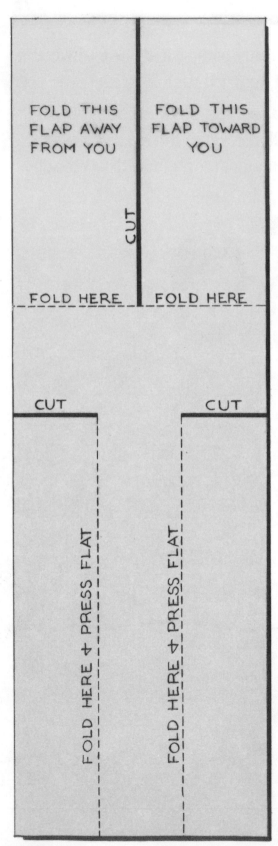

FOLD THIS FLAP AWAY FROM YOU

FOLD THIS FLAP TOWARD YOU

CUT

FOLD HERE | FOLD HERE

CUT | CUT

FOLD HERE & PRESS FLAT | FOLD HERE & PRESS FLAT

Little Wonder

There's a new plane that's a little wonder. Thousands like it have already been made. Yet no one has ever flown in it. The Little Wonder is a paper helicopter that was invented for a paper airplane contest. It stole the show, for it stays in the air longer than any other paper plane. But it doesn't stay up. It comes down slowly, spinning along the way. The spinning keeps it from toppling over and slows its fall.

One of these helicopters kept on spinning all the way to the ground from the roof of a thirty-story building!

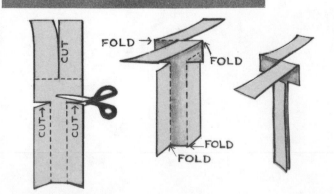

CUT

CUT→ CUT→

FOLD → FOLD

FOLD

FOLD

To make your own Little Wonder, trace the pattern and cut it out of a piece of typing paper.

Hold the helicopter high and let it go. How pretty it looks as it spins! Why does it spin? Air that's trapped under the blades pushes each blade the opposite way. If you bend the blades so that they both point the same way, the helicopter won't spin. Plop! It lands with a crash.

Going Up and Down

In a real helicopter, the blades are curved so that they do both the work of the propeller and of the wings. Tilting them in different ways makes the helicopter go up or come down as the pilot wishes.

These flaps are also called elevators. A plane has flaps on the tail to make it go up or down. When they are down, air is trapped under them. The pressure above is less and the tail is lifted up, tilting the plane. The nose goes down, then the plane starts to dive. But the opposite happens if the tail flaps are up. The pressure above them is greater. The tail is pushed down, and the plane climbs. Since flaps affect lift, they are used during takeoff and landing.

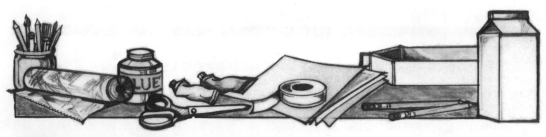

The Flying Flapper

Here's a model you can make with tail flaps that work.

1. Cut a sheet of typewriting paper so that it is 8 inches wide and 8-1/2 inches long.
2. Starting on one side, roll back the paper about 1/2 inch, then roll it back four more times.
3. Fold the paper in half, from bottom to top.
4. Next draw a line across the paper 1 inch from the bottom fold. Crease each half of the paper along the line.

5. Trace the pattern for the cut section on tracing paper.
6. Now cut the paper following the pattern.
7. Open out the plane by bending down each half along the crease.
8. For the flaps, cut a slit 1/2 inch deep and 1-1/4 inches from the outer edge of each part of the tail and you have a flying flapper.

Test the model to see if it flies straight. You may have to adjust it a little. Then try using the tail flaps. Bend them up and the plane climbs. Bend them down and it noses downward.

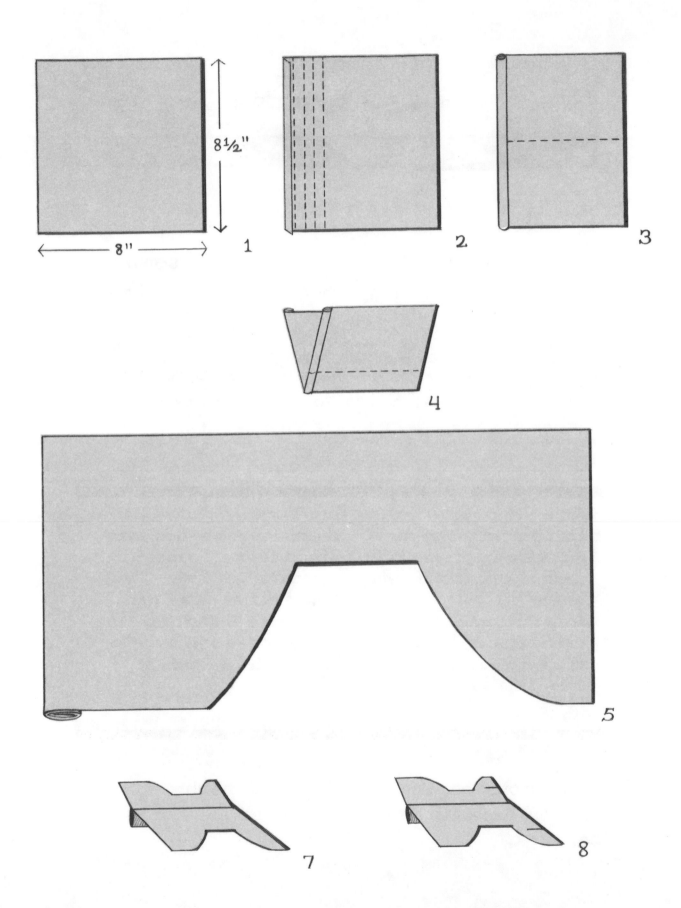

8½"

8"

1

2

3

4

5

7

8

Super Plane

A flying flapper is like a flat bottom sailboat. It is steady but not as fast as a streamlined model. And today, all planes are streamlined.

Here's a streamlined model that's shaped somewhat like the fastest passenger planes. To make this Super Plane use a piece of typewriting paper, cut so that it is 6-1/2 inches by 8 inches.

1. Fold it in half lengthwise.
2. Bring the top corners to the middle and fold them down.
3. Tape the corners to hold them in place.
4. Make a crease on each side of the paper, 1-1/2 inches from the edge, then bend down the paper along these creases.
5. Open out the plane, and cut a slit 3/4 of an inch long along each crease to make tail elevators.

Turn over the plane so the tape is underneath. Now your Super Plane is ready to be tested.

46

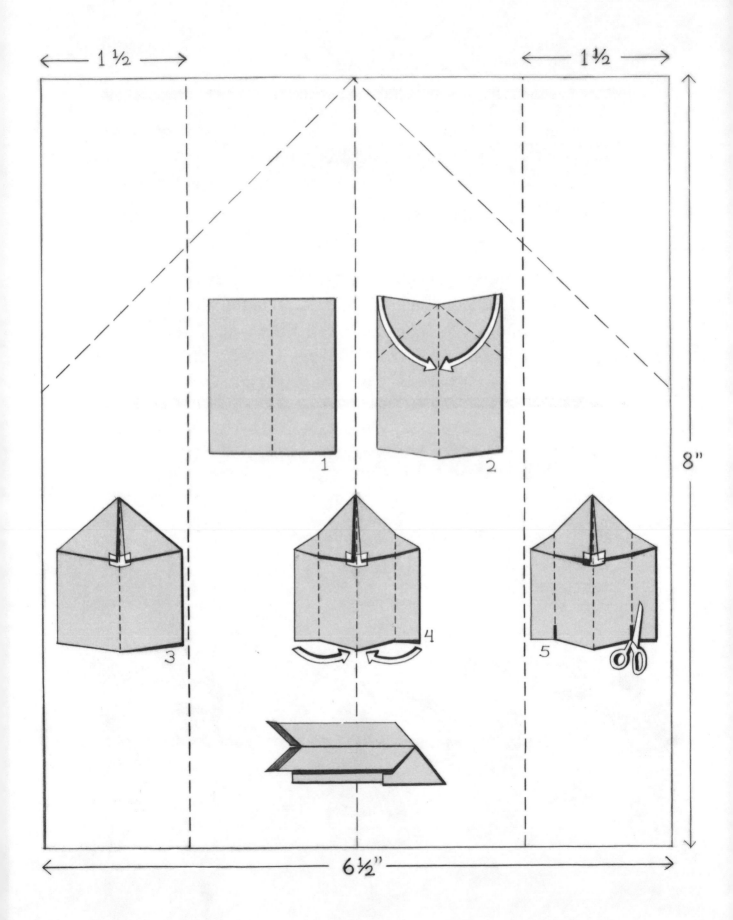

1½

1½

8"

1

2

3

4

5

6½"

When you fly your Super Plane, grasp it with two fingers placed on the tape underneath. It probably will nose dive on the test flight. To balance it, put a dab of modeling clay on the nose.

When the Super Plane is balanced, it will fly straight and fast and go farther than other models.

You can pretend the dab of clay is the pilot. Since you are part of the ground crew, tell the "pilot" to raise the elevators and watch the plane climb. Then see how the plane flies when the elevators are down.

Roundup

Why not get your friends together and give each one a plane to fly. First see which one is the steadiest. Then see which one goes the farthest. Everyone will have fun. . . Science fun!